Contents

Executive Summary 2

I. The U.S. Retirement System 4

II. The Economic Cost of Conflicted Investment Advice 10

    The Evidence on Underperformance 10

    The Effect of Conflicted Advice on Investment Returns 15

    The Dollar Cost of Conflicted Investment Advice 18

III. Alternative Explanations for Underperformance 22

    Is Underperformance the Fair Price of Advice and Other Intangible Benefits? 22

    Does Underperformance Reflect the Characteristics of Households Receiving Conflicted Advice Rather than Conflict Itself? 23

IV. Conclusion 26

References 27

Executive Summary

Americans' retirement income is derived from many sources, including Social Security, traditional pensions, employer-based retirement savings plans such as 401(k)s, and Individual Retirement Accounts (IRAs). While this landscape is familiar today, it reflects a dramatic change from the landscape 40 years ago. The share of working Americans covered by traditional pension plans—which offer a guaranteed income stream in retirement—has fallen sharply. Today, most workers participating in a retirement plan at work are covered by a defined contribution plan, such as a 401(k). Importantly, the income available in retirement from a defined contribution plan depends on both the amount initially saved and the return on those savings. The shift from traditional pensions to defined contribution plans raises important policy issues about investment responsibilities and the roles of individual households, employers, and investment advisers in ensuring the retirement security of Americans.

Defined contribution plans and IRAs are intricately linked, as the overwhelming majority of money flowing into IRAs comes from rollovers from an employer-based retirement plan, not direct IRA contributions. Collectively, more than 40 million American families have savings of more than $7 trillion in IRAs. More than 75 million families have an employer-based retirement plan, own an IRA, or both. Rollovers to IRAs exceeded $300 billion in 2012 and are expected to increase steadily in the coming years. The decision whether to roll over one's assets into an IRA can be confusing and the set of financial products that can be held in an IRA is vast, including savings accounts, money market accounts, mutual funds, exchange-traded funds, individual stocks and bonds, and annuities. Selecting and managing IRA investments can be a challenging and time-consuming task, frequently one of the most complex financial decisions in a person's life, and many Americans turn to professional advisers for assistance. However, financial advisers are often compensated through fees and commissions that depend on their clients' actions. Such fee structures generate acute conflicts of interest: the best recommendation for the saver may not be the best recommendation for the adviser's bottom line.

This report examines the evidence on the cost of conflicted investment advice and its effects on Americans' retirement savings, focusing on IRAs. Investment losses due to conflicted advice result from the incentives conflicted payments generate for financial advisers to steer savers into products or investment strategies that provide larger payments to the adviser but are not necessarily the best choice for the saver.

CEA's survey of the literature finds that:

- Conflicted advice leads to lower investment returns. Savers receiving conflicted advice earn returns roughly 1 percentage point lower each year (for example, conflicted advice reduces what would be a 6 percent return to a 5 percent return).

- An estimated $1.7 trillion of IRA assets are invested in products that generally provide payments that generate conflicts of interest. Thus, we estimate the aggregate annual cost of conflicted advice is about $17 billion each year.

- A retiree who receives conflicted advice when rolling over a 401(k) balance to an IRA at retirement will lose an estimated 12 percent of the value of his or her savings if drawn down over 30 years. If a retiree receiving conflicted advice takes withdrawals at the rate possible absent conflicted advice, his or her savings would run out more than 5 years earlier.

- The average IRA rollover for individuals 55 to 64 in 2012 was more than $100,000; losing 12 percent from conflicted advice has the same effect on feasible future withdrawals as if $12,000 was lost in the transfer.

The conclusions of this report are based on a careful review of the relevant academic literature but, as with any such analysis, are subject to uncertainty. However, this uncertainty should not mask the essential finding of this report: conflicted advice leads to large and economically meaningful costs for Americans' retirement savings. Even a far more conservative estimate of the investment losses due to conflicted advice, such as half of a percentage point, would indicate annual losses of more than $8 billion. On the other hand, if conflicted advice affects a larger portion of IRA assets than the $1.7 trillion considered here—or if the estimate were extended to other forms of retirement savings—the total annual cost would exceed $17 billion.

I.   The U.S. Retirement System

Americans' retirement income comes from many sources. Social Security provides a basic foundation for retirement security. Traditional pensions, employer-based retirement savings plans such as 401(k)s, and Individual Retirement Accounts (IRAs) allow workers to set aside additional earnings explicitly designated for retirement in a tax-advantaged way. (Table 1 provides an overview of these forms of savings.) Other savings, whether in a bank account or a home, provide additional resources that can be tapped in retirement. While this landscape is familiar today, it reflects a dramatic change from the landscape 40 years ago. The share of working Americans covered by traditional pension plans—which offer a guaranteed income stream in retirement—has fallen sharply. Today the majority of workers participating in a retirement plan at work are covered by a defined contribution plan, such as a 401(k).

Table 1. Select Forms of Tax-Preferred Retirement Savings[1]

Type of Plan	Description
Defined Benefit (DB) Plan	Traditional pensions that provide a guaranteed payment for life. Benefits typically determined according to a formula involving some combination of age, earnings, and tenure.
Defined Contribution (DC) Plan	Retirement savings plans that allow employee and/or employer contributions. Benefits depend on both the amount saved and the investment returns net of fees on those assets. Workers bear the risk associated with asset returns. Examples include 401(k)s, 403(b)s, the Federal Thrift Savings Plan, and profit-sharing plans.
Individual Retirement Account (IRA)	Retirement savings plans independent of employment that allow individual contributions. Benefits depend on both the amount saved and the investment returns net of fees on those assets. Individual savers bear the risk associated with asset returns.

---

[1] This report uses the term defined contribution plan to refer to employer-based defined contribution retirement plans (i.e. excluding IRAs).

Figure 1 shows the composition of Americans' tax-preferred retirement savings for the period 1978 to 2013. In 1978, traditional pensions accounted for nearly 70 percent of all retirement assets. Defined contribution plans accounted for less than 20 percent and IRAs accounted for only 2 percent. Annuities accounted for the remainder.[2] By the end of 2013, traditional pensions accounted for only 35 percent of retirement assets, a decrease of 32 percentage points; defined contribution plans and IRAs accounted for more than half of all retirement assets.

This widely discussed shift from traditional pensions to defined contribution plans and IRAs raises important policy issues. In a traditional pension, investment decisions are largely handled by professional managers. In an IRA, investment decisions are almost entirely left to the individual saver. Defined contribution plans, such as 401(k)s, reflect a middle ground where employers may automatically enroll workers in particular default products and may provide workers with access to various forms of advice, but may also provide a large menu of options and nearly unrestricted choice of investment products (Vanguard 2014).

This shift in investment responsibility has coincided with an explosion in the investment options and trading platforms available. The period since 1974 has seen the advent and proliferation of index mutual funds, discount brokerage, exchange-traded funds, online trading, and more. The number and complexity of the products available can make financial decisionmaking difficult (Campbell 2006, Lusardi and Mitchell 2007). Moreover, an abundance of investment options and the way in which investment decisions are framed may challenge financial decisionmaking and lead to worse outcomes for savers (Iyengar et al. 2004, Benartzi et al. 2009). All of these factors in combination have led to an increasing role for financial advice. According to one survey, roughly half of traditional IRA-owning households have a retirement strategy created with the help of a professional financial adviser (Holden and Schrass 2015).

---

[2] In Figure 1, the annuities category excludes annuities held by IRAs, 403(b) plans, 457 plans, and private pension funds.

Table 2: Sources of Investment Advice

Adviser	Description	Legal Standard
Registered Investment Advisers (RIAs)	Receives compensation in exchange for giving investment advice. May also manage a portfolio for clients.	Fiduciary duty to client, including a duty of loyalty and a duty of care. Must serve the best interest of the client.
Broker Dealers (brokers)	Makes trades for a fee or commission. A broker makes trades for a client's account, while a dealer makes trades for his or her own account.	Recommendations must be suitable for a client's investment profile taking into account factors such as age, income, net worth, and investment goals.
Other Potential Sources	Examples include friends, family, bankers, insurance agents, accountants, and lawyers.	Standards vary.

Retirement savers may obtain investment advice from a range of sources, including two primary groups of professionals: brokers and registered investment advisers (RIAs). Table 2 summarizes select sources of investment advice.[3] In addition to investment and asset allocation recommendations, these advisers may provide overall savings advice, tax planning, estate planning, advice on claiming Social Security, and other services. In this report, we use "financial adviser" broadly to include all kinds of professionals providing advice, not just RIAs.

Two important ways in which advisers differ are (i) the legal and conduct standards that their advice must meet and (ii) the ways in which they are compensated for the advice they provide. For example, advice provided by RIAs must serve the best interest of their clients and satisfy duties of loyalty and care. Brokers' recommendations must be suitable for the client taking into account factors such as age and income. Moreover, only registered investment advisers are permitted to give holistic advice, while brokers are restricted to providing incidental advice (Securities and Exchange Commission (SEC) 2011). However, individual advisers can switch back and forth between the two regimes as they engage in different activities, a practice known as dual hatting. As a result, consumers may not know which legal or conduct regime applies to the advice they are receiving at any moment.

The distinctions between the relevant legal standards are important, but they also interact with an important second difference between advisers: differences in the ways in which they are compensated for the advice provided. The key difference is between those advisers who receive conflicted payments and those who do not. Conflicted payments are payments to the adviser that depend on the actions taken by the advisee. For example, an adviser may receive an annual payment for each dollar invested in certain products. Advisers who do not accept conflicted payments may charge an hourly rate, a percentage of assets, or other similar fees that do not directly depend on the investment decisions made by the client. Advisers may also receive both types of compensation: conflicted payments and payments that do not directly depend on their clients' investment decisions.

Advisers accepting conflicted payments face a conflict of interest because the advice that is best for their own bottom line may not be the advice that is best for their customers' savings. These

---

[3] For simplicity, this report refers to both firms and the individual advisers working at those firms as brokers and RIAs.

misaligned interests can arise from a wide range of payment arrangements. Examples include revenue-sharing arrangements and front-end and back-end loads.[4] Table 3 summarizes select forms of conflicted payment arrangements. Advice provided by advisers who accept conflicted payments is referred to as conflicted investment advice. While this report discusses the costs of conflicted investment advice, it is important to keep in mind that many financial advisers hold themselves to high professional standards.

Table 3. Select Types of Payments Generating Conflicts of Interest[5]

Type of Payment	Description of Adviser's Monetary Interest	Potential Consequences
Ongoing revenue-sharing arrangements, including 12b-1 fees	Mutual funds may make ongoing annual payments to advisers based on the advisers' clients' investments, often specified as a percentage of assets. Known by the SEC rule that created them, 12b-1 fees are one example of ongoing revenue-sharing payments.	Creates a financial incentive to direct clients to funds with higher revenue-sharing payments.
Front-end sales load, back-end sales load	Mutual funds may charge investors a fee when an investor buys shares (a front-end load) or sells shares (a back-end load). Most or all of this charge is generally passed on to the advisers selling the product.	Creates a financial incentive to steer investors into funds with higher loads and that pass on a larger portion of that load to advisers. Loads also encourage excessive trading as more trades increase load payments.
Sales targets, payouts	Advisers may receive payouts when they achieve certain sales targets. The payout can vary by asset class and product. In some cases, proprietary products receive higher payouts.	Creates a financial incentive to recommend trading and selling specific products over others based on the schedule of payouts.
Variable commissions	Advisers may receive compensation through commissions for selling individual stocks, insurance products, and other financial products. The amount of the commission can vary across products and asset classes.	Creates a financial incentive to recommend products that generate higher commissions and can encourage excessive trading.

The potential for negative effects of these conflicted payments may be invisible to consumers because they are often unaware of the differences in payment structures and legal standards across advisers and the conflicts they create. Moreover, even when consumers are aware of the differences, they can struggle to know which legal and conduct standard is relevant because advisers can switch between legal and conduct regimes in a given conversation with a client. In surveys, a majority of households reports satisfaction with their advisers and at the same time express confusion and make mistakes about the different titles, legal obligations, and consumer protections that exist in the advice industry (Consumer Financial Protection Bureau (CFPB) 2013, Government Accountability Office (GAO) 2011, Investment Company Institute 1997, SEC 2011). Households also express confusion over the fees that they are charged, reflecting the indirect and sometimes complex pricing of financial advice, which further widens the scope for abuse (Hung et al. 2008).

---

[4] See Financial Industry Regulatory Authority (FINRA) (2013), Howat and Reid (2007), Hung et al. (2008), Turner and Muir (2013), and Prentice (2011) for additional discussion of conflicts.

[5] Conflicted payments are often split between the adviser and the adviser's firm. The allocation between the two affects the size of the financial incentive the payments create, but not generally the nature of the incentive created.

This report focuses on the impact of conflicted advice as it affects IRA owners. Unique features of the IRA market suggest that IRA investors are particularly vulnerable to conflicted advice. First, few individuals contribute to IRAs directly and, instead, most of the money flowing into these accounts accumulates in employer plans and is then rolled over into an IRA when workers change jobs or retire. In 2012, Americans contributed roughly $30 billion to traditional and Roth IRAs. In the same year, they rolled over more than $300 billion to traditional and Roth IRAs. At the point of rollover, savers are making decisions about large quantities of money relative to the sums involved in other more common financial decisions. Many savers may not have full knowledge about their options or a complete understanding of the detailed regulatory differences between their employer plan and an IRA—most notably that advice to roll money out of the plan into an IRA is generally subject to much lower standards of care than advice received in the plan. Moreover, investment fees in a typical IRA may exceed investment fees in a typical 401(k) according to a series of recent GAO reports (GAO 2009, 2011, 2013). While rolling over balances to an IRA makes financial sense for many people, when doing so incurs meaningfully higher fees, it generally does not.

Second, for many Americans making decisions about their IRA investments will be one of the only times they must confront the full set of investment products available in the marketplace and as such will be one of the most complicated savings decisions they will face in their lifetime.[6] Third, IRA assets are largest for older households who may be more vulnerable to losses due to conflicts than other savers (Agarwal et al. 2009, Lusardi et al. 2009). SEC and CFPB reports have found consumer financial protection abuses that are specifically targeted at elderly households (CFPB 2013, SEC 2007).

While many different financial products provide conflicted payments, the analysis in the next section will largely focus on mutual fund assets. This focus is driven by the existence of high-quality empirical evidence on the issue of conflicts of interest for this subset of the market. As shown in Figure 2, mutual funds accounted for about half of all IRA assets in 2013, or roughly $3.5 trillion.[7] However, to the degree that conflicted payments impose costs outside of mutual funds held in IRAs, the total costs imposed would be larger than the headline estimates in this report.

---

[6] According to the Survey of Consumer Finances, nearly half of American families held retirement savings accounts, including DC plans and IRAs, in 2013. Outside of retirement accounts and pension plans, only 14 percent held individual stocks, only 8 percent held mutual funds or other pooled investment funds, and even fewer held CDs, individual bonds, or other managed assets.

[7] Variable annuity mutual fund assets are classified with mutual funds, not annuities.

II.   The Economic Cost of Conflicted Investment Advice

The efficiency losses arising from economic relationships involving conflicting incentives—that is, scenarios where the best financial outcome for each party in an economic relationship differs and the behavior of one or more parties can only be imperfectly monitored—have been studied extensively in the economics literature. These principal-agent problems have been studied across a range of industries and relationships, including medical care (Arrow 1963), corporate management (Jensen and Meckling 1976), performance management (Holmstrom 1982), and the mutual fund industry (Chen et al. 2013).

This report focuses on quantifying the impact of conflicting incentives in the particular case of financial advisers providing conflicted advice to IRA account holders. To do so, it turns to the empirical literature that examines conflicted payments and investment products characterized by conflicted payments. Numerous empirical studies, summarized in Table 4, identify the many costs that result. Most of the studies in the literature summarize their results in terms of underperformance: the amount by which investment returns for affected products fall short of a suitably-defined comparison group.

In the academic literature, practices vary in whether investment returns are presented before (gross) or after (net) expenses have been taken into account and in exactly which expenses are subtracted before reporting the net return. CEA's estimated cost of conflict reflects the impact of conflicted advice on a saver's net return. In the discussion of the empirical evidence in this section, underperformance is often expressed in basis points. Basis points provide a convenient rescaling of percentage points for use when discussing numbers close to 1 percentage point: 1 basis point is equal to 0.01 percentage points, and 100 basis points is 1 percentage point.

This section of the report first reviews the relevant academic literature and then applies the results found in that literature to estimate the effect of conflicted advice on investment returns and the aggregate dollar cost of conflicted investment advice.

The Evidence on Underperformance

A natural place to begin estimating the costs of conflicted investment advice is with a comparison of the investment returns for mutual funds sold through intermediaries and characterized by conflicts of interest with the investment returns for funds sold directly to savers and generally not providing conflicted payments. Importantly, the distinction between these two groups of funds is not identical to the distinction between funds purchased with advice and those without. Savers purchasing funds sold directly to the public may be receiving advice (for example, from a fee-only adviser). Research making this comparison consistently finds that funds characterized by conflicted payments significantly underperform funds sold directly to savers.

Bergstresser et al. (2009) compare the performance of funds sold through intermediaries that tend to offer conflicted payments with that of funds sold directly to savers, where conflicts of interest are significantly weaker. They find that funds sold through intermediaries deliver lower risk-adjusted returns. The researchers examine returns net of operating expenses, but do not include the costs of marketing and selling fund shares such as loads and 12b-1 fees (defined above). Since loads and 12b-1 fees are primary sources of compensation for the intermediaries recommending the funds, the authors' finding indicates that it is not merely the cost of paying those intermediaries that leads to underperformance. During the period covered by the study, the annual returns on domestic equity funds sold through intermediaries were 77 basis points lower than the returns of observationally equivalent direct-sold funds. The annual returns on bond funds sold through intermediaries were 90 basis points lower than equivalent direct-sold funds. The authors estimate that this underperformance amounted to $4.6 billion in 2004.[8]

Del Guercio and Reuter (2014) corroborate the result in Bergstresser et al. (2009): direct-sold funds outperform funds sold through intermediaries, a difference they estimate to be 115 basis points per year. Moreover, looking just at funds characterized by conflicted payments, the authors find that actively-managed funds sold through intermediaries, which comprise the vast majority of all funds sold through intermediaries and feature larger conflicted payments, underperform lower-fee, passively-managed funds sold through intermediaries by 112 to 132 basis points per year; this result does not extend to funds that are sold directly to savers. In other words, underperformance among actively-managed funds is limited to the segment of the mutual fund market where the conflicted payments are the largest. The authors conclude that this result "likely reflect[s] an agency conflict between brokers and their clients" as both actively-managed and passively-managed funds sold through intermediaries provide the same portfolio management and advisory services but provide different payments to the adviser.

These first two studies compare investment returns for funds that tend to make conflicted payments with those that do not. One limitation of this type of comparison is that it may incorporate differences other than the presence of conflicted advice between the types of investors purchasing funds through these two sources. For instance, investors purchasing funds through intermediaries may be more risk-averse and less experienced with investing than those buying direct-sold shares from a mutual fund sponsor. Failing to account for such differences may potentially overstate or understate the losses due to conflicts of interest. However, results from another strand of research that is not affected by this limitation find broadly similar patterns.

In one study, Chalmers and Reuter (2014) compare the performance of accounts in an Oregon workplace retirement plan when plan participants lose access to conflicted advisers. They find that participants who would have otherwise used conflicted advisers when available were disproportionately more likely to rely on the plan's default investment options in their absence, and that those default investment options performed better than the portfolios of those receiving conflicted advice. In the authors' words, "brokers significantly increased annual fees, significantly decreased annual after-fee returns, and slightly increased risk-taking relative to the counterfactual portfolio" (that is, the default investment option). The estimated magnitude of underperformance in this study is large: 298 basis points relative to the plan's default investment option. A portion of this

---

[8] The authors find outperformance of foreign equity funds, but this result is attributable to a small number of large funds sold through a single fund family.

large underperformance estimate is explained by a higher exposure to risky assets in broker clients' portfolios at a time when risky assets performed poorly. The authors also estimate underperformance between portfolios selected on the basis of conflicted advice and those that are not after controlling for various measures of investor traits, and find that these portfolios still underperform by approximately 125 basis points. Similarly, researchers examining retail investment advice in Canada and Germany, where the legal regimes differ but advisers also derive substantial compensation from conflicted payments, find that advised accounts underperform by more than 150 basis points (Foerster et al. 2014, Hackethal et al. 2012a).

Conflicted payments can also lead to underperformance as a result of poor timing in investment decisions. Studies that compare the performance of mutual funds do not necessarily capture this effect, which results from the timing of individual investors' decisions to buy and sell. While poor timing in investment decisions, referred to as market mis-timing, exists for reasons other than conflicted payments, conflicted payments can exacerbate the problem as trading strategies with poor timing may generate higher conflicted payments. Friesen and Sapp (2007) estimate that timing issues from all sources could lead to 100 to 200 basis points of annual underperformance and that these losses appear to be larger among a particular group of funds (load funds) offering conflicted payments. Other research also suggests that conflicted advisers often do not steer clients away from excessive trading, another source of investment losses due to poor timing (Hackethal et al. 2012b).

Table 4. Evidence on the Impact of Conflicted Investment Advice

Study	Impact of Conflict	Discussion
Bergstresser et al. (2009)	Lower returns, higher fees	Broker-sold equity, bond, and money market funds underperform corresponding direct-sold funds by 14 to 90 basis points between 1996 and 2004 before accounting for distribution fees that provide compensation for the adviser. Results also show that compensation to advisers is positively associated with net inflows. Study finds little evidence of superior asset allocation or market timing abilities among advisers.
Chalmers and Reuter (2014)	Lower returns, higher fees, biased advice	Investors in a university-sponsored retirement plan receiving conflicted advice underperform self-directed investors and a counterfactual target-date fund by 125 and 298 basis points, respectively. Within the portfolios of those receiving conflicted advice, fund flows are sensitive to the level of fees, with a 50 basis point increase in broker fees corresponding to a 17.2 percentage point higher allocation to the fund with higher fees. Advisers also steer investors away from high-fee funds when those fees do not benefit the advisers.
Christoffersen et al. (2013)	Biased advice, lower returns, higher fees	Between 1993 and 2009, among mutual funds with loads or revenue-sharing, higher payments to advisers lead to higher inflows, suggesting that advisers' recommendations are biased by the payments they receive. Net returns are approximately 50 basis points lower for every 100 basis points of loads that are shared with advisers.
Del Guercio and Reuter (2014)	Lower returns, higher fees	Actively managed broker-sold mutual funds earn returns 112 to 132 basis points lower than passively managed broker-sold funds, after accounting for distribution fees that provide compensation for the adviser. The authors conclude that this underperformance likely reflects an agency conflict between advisers and their clients.
Foerster et al. (2014)	Lower returns, higher fees, inappropriate risk-taking, advice is not customized	Among Canadian investors, advised portfolios primarily relying on conflicted advice pay 170 basis points more than a lifecycle fund but experience worse market timing and fund selection. Advisers encourage additional risk-taking, but the gain in returns is offset by the higher fees charged by the adviser, leaving the investor with lower risk-adjusted performance than with a lifecycle fund or passive index.
Friesen and Sapp (2007)	Market mis-timing	Investors in load funds experience larger losses (194 basis points) from market mis-timing than those in no-load funds (96 basis points). Losses for both groups are relative to a buy-and-hold strategy.
GAO (2011)	Inappropriate rollovers	In a review of the market, certain advisers' compensation can range from $6,000 to $9,000 if an employer-based plan participant were to purchase an IRA but only $50 to $100 if the same participant were to remain in the plan.
Hackethal et al. (2012a)	Lower returns, higher turnover	Clients of a German brokerage and a German bank receiving advice from advisers primarily compensated through conflicted payments earn lower net returns not justified by reduced risk. Clients' accounts also exhibited higher turnover.
Hackethal et al. (2012b)	Excessive trading, biased advice, higher fees	Investors receiving conflicted advice from a German retail bank between 2005 and 2007 trade more heavily, are more likely to purchase "incentivized" products (e.g. funds with higher loads), and generate higher bank revenues, holding investor characteristics, including financial sophistication, constant.
Mullainathan et al. (2012)	Market mis-timing, higher fees, inappropriate diversification, asset misallocation	In 284 mystery shopper visits to financial advisers, a majority of advisers recommend investment strategies that are in line with their financial interests, such as return chasing and buying actively managed funds. Moreover, advisers steer clients away from low-fee, passively managed portfolios toward higher-fee products.

The studies reviewed so far in this section provide a consistently negative view of the risk-adjusted, post-fee performance of portfolios invested according to conflicted advice but they do not directly link the extent of the underperformance to the magnitude of the conflicted payments. To establish the direct link between conflicts of interest and underperformance, we turn to another set of results in the academic literature. In one study, researchers connected the payments an intermediary receives for selling a particular mutual fund to underperformance (Christoffersen et al. 2013). Comparing data on flows and performance for mutual funds that have unusually high or low payments to intermediaries, the researchers find that inflows are larger for funds with unusually high payments and smaller for those with unusually low payments. Put somewhat differently, if two funds appear otherwise identical but one shares a higher portion of load payments with advisers, the amount of money flowing into that fund will tend to be higher. The authors also find that higher revenue-sharing payments lead to greater inflows. These results provide direct evidence that two important sources of conflicts—namely, load payments and revenue sharing—bias investment recommendations.

Further, the authors find that unusually high or low load-sharing payments lead to unusually low or high performance, respectively. That is, funds with unusually high payments to intermediaries tend to generate unusually low returns.[9] In particular, the average conflicted payment to certain advisers in their data "corresponds to a 1.13% reduction in annual performance" after fees.

The finding that conflicted payments drive investment decisions is corroborated by evidence presented in Chalmers and Reuter (2014). The researchers find that fund flows are sensitive to the level of fees more generally, concluding that a 50 basis point increase in adviser fees corresponds to a 17.2 percentage point higher allocation to the fund. This study also finds evidence that advisers steer investors away from high-fee funds when those fees do not benefit the adviser.

The studies discussed to this point analyze the impact of conflicted payments on mutual fund flows and performance. An alternative perspective on advice can be obtained by examining how advisers treat individuals and assessing the degree to which their recommendations are motivated by the payments they receive. In a mystery shopper study, researchers sent hypothetical investors to financial advisers largely reliant on conflicted payments for their compensation to investigate the type of advice provided (Mullainathan et al. 2012). The mystery shoppers presented four portfolios to advisers: a return-chasing portfolio, an employer stock portfolio, a diversified low-fee portfolio, and a cash portfolio. The study finds that advisers recommend a change to the current investment strategy in about 60 percent of cases when the client had a return-chasing portfolio and in about 85 percent of cases in which the client had a diversified low-fee portfolio. The authors conclude that advisers "seem to support strategies that result in more transactions and higher management fees," even when clients appear to hold the optimal portfolio.

---

[9] While the authors do not find a statistically significant effect of unusually high or low revenue-sharing payments on performance, their point estimate is negative, consistent with—though not dispositive of—reduced performance resulting from unusually high revenue-sharing payments as well.

In the U.S. retirement system, a particularly important financial decision occurs when employees who participate in a workplace retirement plan change jobs or retire and must decide what to do with their existing savings. The options at this point typically include leaving their savings in the current plan, rolling them over into a new employer's plan, or rolling them over into an IRA. However, advisers may recommend inappropriate rollovers to plan participants to collect fees for managing the assets. According to a recent GAO report, certain advisers could earn $6,000 to $9,000 if a plan participant were to purchase an IRA but only $50 to $100 if the same participant were to invest within the employer plan (GAO 2011). Recent analyses have found that plan participants are frequently encouraged to roll over funds to an IRA with minimal knowledge of the participant's financial situation, without acknowledging other options available, and without offering significant discussion of fees (GAO 2013).

The Effect of Conflicted Advice on Investment Returns

As discussed above and seen in Table 4, academic research identifies several ways in which conflicted advice affects investment performance. Because the studies reviewed in this report examine different, partially overlapping aspects of conflict and because they vary in the extent to which their effects are directly attributed to conflict, it would not be appropriate to simply sum or average the estimates to obtain a single overall estimate of the effect of conflicted advice. But taken together, the evidence suggests that conflicted advice leads to underperformance of roughly 100 basis points per year. Here, we outline the various considerations that lead us to this estimate.

Our approach starts from a study that directly examines the relationship between payments to advisers and performance. Christoffersen et al. (2013) conclude that the magnitude of losses from conflict corresponding to the fund with the average load-sharing payment is 113 basis points, which is in line with our estimate. However, whether this estimate is a good indicator of conflict-driven underperformance today depends on the relative magnitudes of at least three adjustments that may either push the estimate higher or lower. First, average loads may be somewhat lower today than the average during the period studied in the paper (1993 to 2009), which would lead us to adjust the underperformance estimate down. Second, this estimate does not factor in the direct impact of the additional load payment the investor incurs as a result of the recommendation to invest in funds with higher loads, which would lead to an upward adjustment. Third, the authors estimate underperformance for the first year in which the funds are purchased rather than underperformance for every year that the saver holds the fund. Adjusting for this detail would increase or decrease the underperformance estimate depending on whether the effect grows or decays in subsequent years. While the literature provides little formal guidance on this specific question, the authors control for cyclical fluctuations that might lead their underperformance estimate to differ depending on business cycle conditions. In addition, studies that estimate underperformance in portfolios, where a fund's performance can be tracked beyond the first year of ownership, find annual estimates of underperformance over time that are consistent with the first-year effect (Hackethal et al. 2012b, Chalmers and Reuter 2014, Foerster et al. 2014). Both of these explanations provide suggestive evidence that the one-year estimate of underperformance in Christoffersen et al. (2013) is a reasonable approximation for the persistent effect. Taking all three of these adjustments into consideration leads us to conclude that 100 basis points is a plausible estimate around which to center the magnitude of underperformance.

An alternative approach would build up the estimate from separate estimates for each of the ways conflicted investment advice can lead to underperformance: excessive fees, excessive trading, market mis-timing, and so forth. However, there is insufficient precision in the literature to separately estimate each of these sources of underperformance in such a calculation—although the individual estimates cited above support an aggregate estimate of 100 basis points in that many of the individual estimates in the literature are 100 basis points or higher.

As with any attempt to assign a specific value to an unobservable quantity, there is uncertainty in this estimated cost of conflict. For example, if a large fraction of market mis-timing reflects the impact of conflicted advice, the cost could be larger. If the impact of unusually high or low conflicted payments on performance (the basis for the Christoffersen et al. (2013) analysis) differs systematically from the impact of expected differences in conflicted payments, the cost of conflict could be either over or understated.

The definition of underperformance used in this report is broad and encompasses a wide range of channels through which returns can suffer, including high fees, high trading costs, poor market timing, and increased risk exposure without increased returns. Because these sources of underperformance reflect a mix of implicit and explicit costs that may not appear on any account statement, it can be difficult to see how they reduce the returns a worker earns on his retirement savings. This box provides a simplified example to illustrate what underperformance means in practice.

Consider two potential options for a worker who has recently changed jobs: leaving her 401(k) balance in the old plan or rolling over to an IRA. (In many cases, the worker could also choose to roll over the balance to a retirement plan at the new job. For simplicity, this example ignores this option as well as the option to withdraw the balance from the account.)

Suppose the worker's previous employer ran a large 401(k) plan with several low-cost investment options, and the worker was invested in an index fund holding a mix of stocks and bonds. Suppose further that the expected return for the fund's portfolio before accounting for any expenses is 6.5 percent. In practice, it is not possible for the worker to earn this return because it is the return that would be earned if the fund didn't need to pay anyone to make trades, manage customer service, process employee contributions to the plan, and so on. The trading costs for index funds tend to be quite low; this example assumes they lower the saver's expected return by 5 basis points. The fund's management and operating expenses reduce the returns by another 20 basis points. Finally, the costs of administering the 401(k) plan itself reduce returns by another 25 basis points. Altogether, these expenses reduce the return by 50 basis points. Thus, each year that the worker holds this investment, she can expect to earn 6.5 percent minus 0.5 percent for a net gain of 6.0 percent (see Table). Of course, in any particular year, returns may be higher or lower depending on the performance of the market.

	401(k)	Recommended IRA
Portfolio's gross return	6.50%	6.50%
- Trading costs	0.05%	0.20%
- Mutual fund expenses	0.20%	1.30%
- 401(k) plan expenses	0.25%	0.00%
Saver's net return	6.00%	5.00%

Now suppose the worker receives a recommendation to roll over her balance to an IRA and invest in a higher cost mutual fund with an investment strategy that involves more frequent trading. This type of recommendation can arise because the person making the recommendation receives higher compensation if the worker rolls over her balance to an IRA than if she keeps her funds in her 401(k). However, unless the fund involves a significantly different risk profile than the index fund, the expected return will likely be quite similar.

This example simplifies and assumes the IRA investment matches the risk characteristics of the 401(k) investment and earns an identical expected return before accounting for any costs. Yet the fund's frequent trading strategy results in significantly higher trading costs, reducing returns by 20 basis points rather than 5. In addition, the mutual fund's management and operating expenses are 130 basis points, up from 20. However, in the IRA the worker would no longer need to pay the 401(k) plan management fees, which reduced returns by 25 basis points. In combination, the costs for the IRA investment reduce earnings by 150 basis points annually. Thus, each year the saver holds this investment she can expect to earn 5 percent.

In this example, conflicted advice reduces the expected return on a saver's investment each year from 6 percent to 5 percent. Over time, reduced annual returns add up to significant reductions in a saver's potential retirement savings. Suppose the worker's rollover occurred at age 45 and she expects to retire at 65. The 1 percentage point reduction in the expected annual return leads to a reduction in the expected value of her savings from this account at age 65 of 17 percent.

Lower returns likewise reduce the value of accumulated savings in the retirement years. For a saver who plans to take withdrawals over a 30-year period (beginning immediately), the lower return resulting from conflicted advice will require her to reduce the annual withdrawals from the account by 12 percent compared to what she could have withdrawn each year absent conflicts of interest.[a] Alternatively, if she chooses to withdraw the amount that could have been withdrawn each year when earning the higher return, she would run out of money more than five years earlier.

These losses in retirement come on top of the losses in the pre-retirement period for workers with a mid-career rollover. For the saver in this example who rolls over her 401(k) balance at 45, the combined effect of a 17 percent loss leading up to retirement and a 12 percent loss after retirement is an overall loss of more than 25 percent. That is, as a result of conflicted investment advice, the feasible retirement withdrawals for this saver fall by more than 25 percent compared to what would have been possible with unconflicted advice.

a. Withdrawal computations assume constant inflation-adjusted withdrawals and an inflation rate of 2 percent.

The Dollar Cost of Conflicted Investment Advice

Translating the effect of conflicted advice on investment returns into a dollar cost requires an estimate of the value of assets invested according to conflicted advice. We can then multiply the estimated value of affected assets by the effect of conflict on investment returns to obtain the total dollar cost of conflict.

Implementing this straightforward computation, however, is complicated by the number of different ways in which advice can be delivered, the methodological differences across empirical studies, and the limitations of the publicly available data. Systematic, quantitative evidence on the effects of conflict is richest for mutual funds. As a result, a conservative approach would apply the effect of conflicted advice on investment returns obtained above only to a pool of mutual fund assets affected by conflicts of interest. A less conservative approach would apply the cost of conflicted advice obtained for mutual funds to all assets affected by conflicts of interest, using the underperformance among mutual funds as indicative of the effect across investment products.

We identify three potential estimates of IRA assets subject to conflicted investment advice. The first—and narrowest—estimate corresponds to mutual funds with loads in IRAs. While using load funds as an indicator of conflicted payments is imperfect, as such funds can waive loads for certain investors and a saver could simply choose to invest in such a fund even without receiving advice, it almost certainly underestimates the pool of assets affected by conflicted advice by excluding an extremely large range of products, including variable annuities and no-load funds, that could be recommended on the basis of conflicted payments. We estimate the value of load funds in IRAs by multiplying the share of load funds among non-institutional mutual fund assets at the end of 2013 by the total value of mutual fund assets in IRAs. This yields an estimate of $1.05 trillion.[10]

Table 5. Estimates of IRA Assets Affected by Conflicted Investment Advice

	IRA Assets Affected	Asset Composition
Low	$1.05 trillion	Value of load mutual funds in IRAs
Middle	$1.66 trillion	Value of load mutual funds and annuities in IRAs
High	$3.26 trillion	Value of advised IRA assets

The second estimate of IRA assets invested according to conflicted investment advice is the combination of load funds and variable annuity mutual funds in IRAs. (Variable annuities often provide conflicted payments such as differential commissions and revenue-sharing payments.) This estimate captures a larger share of potentially affected assets and maintains a focus on the mutual fund products that were the focus of the empirical research reviewed above. We estimate this pool in the same manner as the pool above, taking the share of load funds and variable annuity mutual funds among non-institutional mutual fund assets and multiplying by the value of mutual fund assets in IRAs. This yields an estimate of $1.66 trillion.

The third estimate of IRA assets invested according to conflicted investment advice is a conservative estimate of IRA assets for which individuals receive any advice. We compute this by multiplying the value of IRA assets by the share of traditional IRA owners who consulted a professional financial adviser when creating a retirement strategy.[11] This yields an estimate of $3.26 trillion. While this estimate likely underestimates the value of IRA assets invested according to professional advice, as large accounts are likely disproportionately advised, it likely overestimates the value invested according to conflicted advice as some advice does not involve conflicts of interest. Moreover, applying the estimated cost of conflict in this manner requires extending results obtained from analysis of mutual fund performance to many other kinds of assets. Despite these limitations of the analysis, it is important to understand the potential cost of conflict across all assets rather than assuming that conflicts of interest do not affect assets other than mutual funds. Finally, as this report

---

[10] The dollar value of load funds and non-institutional mutual fund assets in 2013 is from Investment Company Institute (ICI) (2014). The total value of mutual fund assets in IRAs at the end of 2013 is from ICI's "The U.S. Retirement Market, Third Quarter 2014" available at http://www.ici.org/research/stats/retirement.

[11] The share of IRA owners relying on professional retirement advice is from Holden and Schrass (2015).

focuses on quantifying the cost of conflicted advice on IRA savings, the estimates are inherently conservative as they exclude a substantial fraction of all savings.

Each of these three approaches has advantages and disadvantages. Focusing on load funds in IRAs limits attention to a set of investments most closely related to those analyzed in the academic research reviewed above. Moreover, it restricts attention to a pool of assets highly likely to be invested according to conflicted advice. And, by virtue of excluding all assets other than load funds, it likely underestimates the relevant pool of assets even though some load fund assets may not be subject to conflict. However, this conservative approach likely substantially understates the total cost of conflict by ignoring conflicted advice to invest in other products. The second estimate's focus on load funds and variable annuity mutual funds remains close to the subject of academic studies but encompasses a somewhat wider array of products. Finally, the full set of IRA assets subject to advice likely overstates the cost of conflicted advice for IRA owners as some of the advice may be provided by advisers who do not receive conflicted payments. Moreover, it applies empirical evidence obtained from studies primarily of mutual funds to a context where it may be less relevant. However, as noted above, the costs of conflicted advice extend beyond the IRA market considered here.

Applying the estimated effect of conflict on investment returns to the intermediate estimate of affected assets yields an annual cost of conflict for retirement savers of $17 billion. Importantly, while the precise magnitude of the underperformance depends on the point estimates chosen, the scale of the loss does not. Even if the effect of conflict on investment returns is half as large, retirement savers are losing $8.5 billion per year. On the other hand, if the pool of affected assets is better approximated by the high estimate above, retirement savers are losing $33 billion per year.

IS THE CURRENT SYSTEM THE ONLY WAY FOR AMERICANS WITH MODEST SAVINGS TO OBTAIN ADVICE?

This analysis concludes that conflicted advice costs Americans about $17 billion in foregone retirement earnings each year. The costly effects of conflicted advice may be particularly relevant for Americans with modest retirement savings, as historically they have relied on types of advice often subject to conflicts. Due to these patterns, some observers have asserted that advising structures using conflicted payments are the only way that savers with lower balances can obtain advice and that without such advice the adequacy of their retirement savings would suffer. This argument, however, falls short in multiple ways and overlooks channels that could provide high-quality, conflict-free advice to moderate-income savers at the same cost as conflicted advising structures.

First, advisers can provide the same quality of advice while receiving non-conflict-based payments as they can when receiving a payment of equal amount based in conflict. The cost of advice depends primarily on the resources necessary to provide it—the adviser's time, IT infrastructure, and other inputs—rather than the form of the adviser's compensation. Thus, an adviser receiving payment through non-conflicted structures should be able to provide advice at the same cost as an adviser receiving conflicted payments, as long as the inputs in time and infrastructure are equal. If advisers serving moderate-income Americans can remain profitable regardless of whether they receive conflicted or non-conflicted compensation, one would expect the number of advisers working with lower-balance savers to remain the same regardless of whether conflict-based payment systems remain in use.

Second, the prevalence of conflicted payments today may actually interfere with low-balance savers' ability to get advice. Ongoing developments in the financial industry are sharply reducing the cost of advice, but it may be difficult for new entrants providing quality, unconflicted, low-cost advice to compete on price when other advice erroneously appears to be free. Therefore the prevalence of hidden fees and conflicted payments may make it more difficult for low-cost, high-quality alternatives to compete on a level playing field, reducing moderate-income Americans' available options for inexpensive advice. As just one example, new approaches to advice that exploit technological advances are allowing firms to offer personalized advice at costs well below those of traditional advice.

Finally, savers with modest balances today tend to become savers with larger balances tomorrow. According to the Employee Benefit Research Institute, more than 60 percent of IRA contributors in 2010 contributed in at least one of the next two years and nearly 40 percent contributed in every year from 2010 to 2012 (Copeland 2014). A significant motivator for the services provided to low-balance customers today is likely their potential to become higher balance customers in the future. Financial advisers have strong incentives to work with lower-balance savers regardless of whether using conflicted or non-conflicted payment structures.

III. Alternative Explanations for Underperformance

The previous section reviews a range of studies that quantify the costs of conflicted investment advice in terms of underperformance. Some of the most compelling studies examine conflicted payments and advice directly, such as the study by Christoffersen et al. (2013) that finds higher conflicted payments drive increased investment in mutual funds and correspond to underperformance of such funds. Other studies provide evidence that mutual funds that tend to make conflicted payments underperform those that do not. While conflicted payments are a logical explanation for the underperformance identified in this second group of studies, other alternative explanations have been advanced for the finding. In this section, we explore two alternative explanations. Generally speaking, the support in the literature for these alternative explanations is unsatisfying. As a result, although we acknowledge the possibility that factors other than conflicts of interest could be at play, we do not find enough compelling evidence or justification to challenge our conclusion that advisers' conflicts of interest are quantitatively significant and erode households' retirement assets by billions of dollars each year. Moreover, even if these alternative explanations are a factor in generating underperformance in funds that typically make conflicted payments, they would not explain why atypically high conflicted payments generate additional flows and additional underperformance.

Is Underperformance the Fair Price of Advice and Other Intangible Benefits?

Advisers deserve fair compensation for their services. In many cases, their earnings are derived from conflicted payments. Thus, one alternative explanation for underperformance among funds offering conflicted payments is that this underperformance merely reflects the necessary and reasonable compensation for advisers. However, much of the research is careful to exclude fees used to compensate advisers from their underperformance calculation. For example, the baseline results reported in Bergstresser et al. (2009) report underperformance before fees used to provide adviser compensation are taken into account. Thus, it is unlikely that the underperformance reflects the fair price of advice.

Relatedly, given the existence of underperformance in these funds, some question whether investors select such funds for intangible benefits provided by the funds or the advisers that recommend them. However, other research results raise doubts about this explanation. For example, studies find that households are mostly unaware of their advisers' conflicts and compensation arrangements, suggesting they have not built an assessment of those conflicts into their selection of the adviser (Malmendier and Shanthikumar 2007, Mullainathan et al. 2012, SEC 2011). Also, in an experimental setting where fees are made salient, Choi et al. (2010) conclude that investors are unlikely to buy high-fee funds for the bundled services they provide. Lastly, studies document how, in many consumer finance contexts, the opaque pricing of financial products can create opportunities for potential abuses, particularly affecting elderly consumers.[12] All of these considerations suggest that the opaque and complex pricing structures are likely to pose challenges for households.

---

[12] See Engel and McCoy (2002) for a discussion of loan markets; for a focus on elderly individuals in financial markets, see Infogroup/ORC (2010) and SEC (2007).

Does Underperformance Reflect the Characteristics of Households Receiving Conflicted Advice Rather than Conflict Itself?

Households differ in their financial characteristics, such as net worth and income; their knowledge of personal finance; and the competing demands on their time. Customers purchasing mutual funds characterized by conflicted payments differ modestly from those purchasing mutual funds directly along certain dimensions, such as income and education (Bergstresser et al. 2009). If correlated with their investment needs or abilities, these differences could lead to underperformance among funds characterized by conflicted payments. However, as noted in the original paper, while these differences could easily lead to differences in willingness to pay for advice (in either direction), it is not clear why they would necessarily lead to differences in underperformance after accounting for the fees that provide compensation for the adviser.

Households from all backgrounds fall subject to common behavioral biases, such as over-confidence, over-optimism, and loss aversion. These biases often lead to lower investment returns because they lead households to (i) trade excessively by seeking active management or chasing returns, (ii) sell winning investments while holding losing investments, (iii) overweight past returns, or (iv) under-diversify.[13] If households affected by these biases disproportionately hold funds characterized by conflicted payments, it may be the case that these biases, rather than the conflicts of interest among financial advisers, lead to the underperformance.

This second possibility is less directly addressed by papers that focus solely on underperformance at the fund level. However, turning to the other results reviewed above that directly examine financial advice provides insight. For example, Mullainathan et al. (2012) find that in a sample of advisers who predominantly rely on conflicted payments for their income, advisers often recommend substantial changes to portfolios that currently follow best practices and are less likely to recommend changes to portfolios that do not follow best practices when doing so would likely reduce their earnings. This finding raises significant doubts about the extent to which conflicted advice is serving as a brake on behavioral biases.

---

[13] See, for example, Barber and Odean (2000, 2001, 2002, 2013), Benartzi and Thaler (2001), Choi et al. (2011), Calvet et al. (2007).

Do Mandated Disclosures Provide a Solution?

Mandated disclosures are a common regulatory tool for promoting the transparency and comprehension of consumer financial products. Despite their ubiquity, when used to inform savers of the conflicts of interest between them and their advisers, the effects of disclosure by itself are limited and, in many cases, lead to harm and weaker consumer protections. Indeed, many financial advisers already provide disclosures and the evidence discussed in this report suggests that they are not highly effective. Here, we briefly explore some of the challenges with disclosures in the market for financial advice.[a]

Perhaps most importantly, current disclosure practices for IRAs and retail financial investment products lack salience. They are often discussed in fine print sections using legal language or other terms whose meaning may be opaque. It should not be surprising then that investors seldom read financial disclosures, viewing them as meaningless, and therefore do not become informed by them (ICI 2006). Moreover, when disclosures are presented at the point of sale, as is common in many financial transactions, it is often too late for the disclosure to influence investors' decisions, even for financially sophisticated individuals.

Even if disclosures are highly salient, design challenges remain. Research suggests that disclosures are most effective when they simultaneously satisfy three criteria: accessibility, accuracy, and relevance, and it is difficult to simultaneously satisfy these three objectives. Nevertheless, the need to do so is especially acute when the amount of information a consumer needs is vast and when products are complex, as is the case with IRA investments. Because individuals can only process a limited amount of information at one time, it is easy to overload them with too much information, which necessitates hard choices and tradeoffs in what should be disclosed. Given how differently individuals process financial information, the disclosure design must recognize that the same information can easily be interpreted differently by different types of individuals.

Finally, in practice, disclosures of conflicts of interest can actually backfire (Cain et al. 2005, Loewenstein et al. 2011). Research in behavioral economics and psychology demonstrates that when advisers disclose their conflicts, they may be more willing to pursue their own interest over those of their clients and thus give worse advice. Advisees may interpret the disclosure as a sign of honesty and become more likely to follow their advisers' biased advice.

a. For a fuller discussion of mandated disclosures, see Ben-Shahar and Schneider (2011).

INTERNATIONAL POLICY CHANGES TO MITIGATE CONFLICTED ADVICE

Several countries have recently enacted regulations to mitigate conflicts of interest for retail financial products. The United Kingdom and Australia both banned payments from product providers to advisers and increased disclosure requirements. The European Union Markets in Financial Instruments Directive 2 (MiFID 2), scheduled to take effect by early 2017, proposes to ban conflicted payments for certain advisers and requires policies and procedures to ensure that any advisers who accept conflicted payments are properly incentivized to serve clients' interests.[a] The table below summarizes recent international policy changes to address conflicted advice in select countries.[b]

Country	Description
Australia[c]	Banned payments from product providers and conflicted remuneration payments for retail investments and created a statutory duty for advisers to act in the best interest of their clients.
Canada	New regulations, implementation of which began in 2014, require much greater transparency about the direct and indirect costs to the client for each account and details on adviser compensation by clients and product providers.
India	Banned all front loads for mutual fund products beginning in 2009. Implemented heightened requirements to disclose the value and justification for any commission payments to advisers.
Italy	Banned commissions for discretionary portfolio management services beginning in 2007.
Germany	Increased disclosures about the cost of advice and whether advisers are compensated solely through client fees or by payments from service providers.
The Netherlands	Banned all payments by a product issuer to an adviser relating to advice beginning in 2013. The ban applies to investment, insurance, and mortgage and protection (annuity) products.
United Kingdom[d]	Banned conflicted payments, increased education and credentialing standards, and required advisers to disclose whether they make recommendations from a restricted menu of products or across all products beginning in 2013.

a. European Parliament (2014).
b. Information in the table below comes from BlackRock (2014) unless otherwise noted.
c. Australian Securities & Investment Commission (2015).
d. Financial Conduct Authority (2014).

IV.   Conclusion

This report examines the evidence on the cost of conflicted investment advice and its effects on Americans' retirement savings, with a focus on IRAs. CEA's survey of the evidence suggests that conflicted advice reduces investment returns by roughly 1 percentage point for savers receiving that advice. In the aggregate, such savers hold about $1.7 trillion of IRA assets. Thus, we estimate the aggregate annual cost of conflicted advice is about $17 billion each year.

The conclusions of this report are based on a careful review of the relevant academic literature but, as with any such analysis, are subject to uncertainty. However, this uncertainty should not mask the essential finding of this report: conflicted advice leads to large and economically meaningful costs for Americans' retirement savings. Even a far more conservative estimate of the investment losses due to conflicted advice, such as half of a percentage point, would yield annual losses of more than $8 billion. On the other hand, if conflicted advice affects a larger portion of IRA assets than the $1.7 trillion considered here—or if the estimate were extended to other forms of retirement savings—the total annual cost would exceed $17 billion.

References

Agarwal, Sumit, John C. Driscoll, Xavier Gabaix, and David Laibson. 2009. "The Age of Reason: Financial Decisions over the Lifecycle with Implications for Regulation." *Brookings Papers on Economic Activity* 2: 51-117.

Arrow, Kenneth J. 1963. "Uncertainty and the Welfare Economics of Medical Care." *The American Economic Review* 53(5): 941-973.

Australian Securities & Investment Commission. 2015. "FOFA - Background and implementation." Australian Securities & Investment Commission. < http://asic.gov.au/regulatory-resources/financial-services/future-of-financial-advice-reforms/fofa-background-and-implementation/>.

Barber, Brad, and Terrance Odean. 2000. "Trading is Hazardous to Your Wealth: The Common Stock Investment Performance of Individual Investors." *Journal of Finance* LV(2): 773-806.

Barber, Brad, and Terrance Odean. 2001. "Boys will be Boys: Gender, Overconfidence, and Common Stock Investment." *Quarterly Journal of Economics* 116(1): 261-292.

Barber, Brad, and Terrance Odean. 2002. "Online Investors: Do the Slow Die First?" *Review of Financial Studies* 15(2): 455-487.

Barber, Brad, and Terrance Odean. 2013. "The Behavior of Individual Investors." *Handbook of the Economic of Finance* 2(B): 1533-1570.

Benartzi, Shlomo, and Richard H. Thaler. 2001. "Naive Diversification Strategies in Defined Contribution Saving Plans." *American Economic Review* 91(1): 79-98.

Benartzi, Shlomo, Ehud Peleg, and Richard H. Thaler. 2009. "Choice Architecture and Retirement Saving Plans." In Eldar Shafir (Ed.). *The Behavioral Foundations of Policy*. Russell Sage Foundation and Princeton University Press.

Ben-Shahar, Omri, and Carl E. Schneider. 2011. "The failure of mandated disclosure." University of Pennsylvania Law Review, 647-749.

Bergstresser, Daniel, John Chalmers, and Peter Tufano. 2009. "Assessing the Costs and Benefits of Brokers in the Mutual Fund Industry." *The Review of Financial Studies* 22(10): 4129-4156.

BlackRock. 2014. "The Changing Face of European Distribution: A Better Financial Future for Savers?" BlackRock ViewPoints. http://www.blackrock.com/corporate/en-br/literature/whitepaper/viewpoint-european-distribution-may-2014.pdf.

Cain, Daylian M., George Loewenstein, and Don A. Moore. 2005. "The Dirt on Coming Clean: Perverse Effects of Disclosing Conflicts of Interest." The Journal of Legal Studies 34 (1): 1-25.

Calvet, Laurent E., John Y. Campbell, and Paolo Sodini. 2007. "Down or Out: Assessing the Welfare Costs of Household Investment Mistakes." *Journal of Political Economy* 115(October): 707-747.

Campbell, John Y. 2006. "Household Finance." *Journal of Finance* 61(4): 1553-1604.

Chalmers, John, and Jonathan Reuter. 2014. "What is the Impact of Financial Advisers on Retirement Portfolio Choices and Outcomes?" National Bureau of Economic Research Working Paper w18158. https://www2.bc.edu/jonathan-reuter/research/ORP_201405.pdf.

Chen, Joseph, Harrison Hong, Wenxi Jiang, and Jeffrey D. Kubik. 2013. "Outsourcing Mutual Fund Management: Firm Boundaries, Incentives, and Performance." *The Journal of Finance* 68 (2): 523-558.

Choi, James J., David Laibson, and Brigitte C. Madrian. 2010. "Why does the law of one price fail? An experiment on index mutual funds." Review of Financial Studies 23 (4): 1405-1432.

Choi, James J., David Laibson, and Brigitte C. Madrian. 2011. "$100 bills on the sidewalk: Suboptimal investment in 401(k) plans." *Review of Economics and Statistics* 93(3): 748-763.

Christoffersen, Susan E.K., Richard Evans, and David K. Musto. 2013. "What Do Consumers' Fund Flows Maximize? Evidence from Their Brokers' Incentives." *Journal of Finance* 68(1): 201-235.

Consumer Financial Protection Bureau (CFPB). 2013. "Senior Designations for Financial Advisers: Reducing Consumer Confusion and Risks." http://files.consumerfinance.gov/f/201304_CFPB_OlderAmericans_Report.pdf.

Copeland, Craig. 2014. "Individual Retirement Account Balances, Contributions, and Rollovers, 2012; With Longitudinal Results 2010–2012: The EBRI IRA Database." *Employee Benefit Research Institute* 339. http://www.ebri.org/pdf/briefspdf/ebri_ib_399_may14.iras.pdf.

Del Guercio, Diane, and Jonathan Reuter. 2014. "Mutual Fund Performance and the Incentive to Generate Alpha." *The Journal of Finance* 69: 1673-1704.

Engel, Kathleen C., and Patricia A. McCoy. 2002. "A Tale of Three Markets: The Law and Economics of Predatory Lending." *Texas Law Review* 80 (6): 1255.

European Parliament. 2014. "MEPs vote laws to regulate financial markets and curb high-frequency trading." Committee on Economic and Monetary Affairs. http://www.europarl.europa.eu/pdfs/news/expert/infopress/20140411IPR43438/20140411IPR43438_en.pdf

Financial Conduct Authority. 2014. "Retail Distribution Review (RDR)." London. Accessed February 19, 2015. http://www.fca.org.uk/firms/firm-types/sole-advisers/rdr#

Financial Industry Regulatory Authority (FINRA). 2013. "Report on Conflict of Interest." http://www.finra.org/web/groups/industry/@ip/@reg/@guide/documents/industry/p359971.pdf.

Foerster, Stephen, Juhani T. Linnainmaa, Brian T. Melzer, and Alessandro Previtero. 2014. "Retail Financial Advice: Does One Size Fit All?" National Bureau of Economic Research Working Paper 20712.

Friesen, Geoffrey C., and Travis RA Sapp. 2007. "Mutual Fund Flows and Investor Returns: An Empirical Examination of Fund Investor Timing Ability." *Journal of Banking and Finance* 31(9): 2796-2816.

Government Accountability Office (GAO). 2009. "Conflicts of Interest Can Affect Defined Benefit and Defined Contribution Plans." GAO-09-503T. http://www.gao.gov/assets/130/122042.pdf.

—. 2011. "401(K) Plans: Improved Regulation Could Better Protect Participants from Conflicts of Interest." GAO-11-119. http://www.gao.gov/assets/320/315369.html.

—. 2013. "401(K) Plans: Labor and IRS Could Improve the Rollover Process for Participants." GAO-13-30. http://www.gao.gov/assets/660/652881.pdf.

Hackethal, Andreas, Michael Haliassos, and Tullio Jappelli. 2012a. "Financial Advisers: A Case of Babysitters?" *Journal of Banking and Finance* 36(2): 509-524.

Hackethal, Andreas, Roman Inderst, and Steffen Meyer. 2012b. "Trading on Advice." University of Frankfurt. Available at SSRN 1701777.

Holden, Sarah, and Daniel Schrass. 2015. "The Role of IRAs in the U.S. Households' Saving for Retirement, 2014." ICI Research Perspective 21(1). http://www.ici.org/pdf/per21-01.pdf.

Holmstrom, Bengt. 1982. "Moral hazard in teams." *The Bell Journal of Economics* 13(2): 324-340.

Howat, John, and Linda Reid. 2007. "Compensation Practices for Retail Sale of Mutual Funds: the Need for Transparency and Disclosure." *Fordham Journal of Corporate and Financial Law* 12(4): 687-91.

Hung, Angela A., Noreen Clancy, Jeff Dominitz, Eric Talley, Claude Berrebi, and Farrukh Suvankulov. 2008. *Investor and Industry Perspectives on Investment Advisers and Broker-Dealers*. RAND Corporation.

Infogroup/ORC. 2010. "Elder Investment Fraud and Financial Exploitation A Survey Conducted for Investor Protection Trust." *Investor Protection Trust.* Washington, DC. http://www.investorprotection.org/downloads/EIFFE_Survey_Report.pdf

Investment Company Institute (ICI). 1997. "Understanding Shareholders' Use of Information and Advisers." Washington, DC. http://www.ici.org/pdf/rpt_undstnd_share.pdf

—. 2006. "Understanding Investor Preferences for Mutual Fund Information." Washington, DC. http://www.ici.org/pdf/rpt_06_inv_prefs_full.pdf.

—. 2014. "2014 Investment Company Fact Book: A Review of Trends and Activities in the U.S. Investment Company Industry." 54th Edition. http://www.ici.org/pdf/2014_factbook.pdf.

Iyengar, Sheena S., Gur Huberman, and Wei Jiang. 2004. "How Much Choice is Too Tuch? Contributions to 401(k) retirement plans." In Mitchell, Olivia S., and Stephen Utkus (Ed.): *Pension Design and Structure: New Lessons from Behavioral Finance*. Oxford University Press, 83-95.

Jensen, Michael C., and William H. Meckling. 1976. "Theory of the Firm: Managerial Behavior, Agency Costs, and Ownership Structure." Journal of Financial Economics 3(4): 78-79.

Loewenstein, George, Daylian M. Cain, and Sunita Sah. 2011. "The Limits of Transparency: Pitfalls and Potential of Disclosing Conflicts of Interest." The American Economic Review 101(3): 423-428.

Lusardi, Annamaria, and Olivia S. Mitchell. 2007. "Financial Literacy and Retirement Preparedness: Evidence and Implications for Financial Education Programs." Michigan Retirement Research Center Research Working Paper 2006-144.

Lusardi, Annamaria, Olivia S. Mitchell, and Vilsa Curto. 2009. "Financial Literacy and Financial Sophistication among Older Americans." National Bureau of Economic Research Working Paper 15469.

Malmendier, Ulrike, and Devin Shanthikumar. 2007. "Are Small Investors Naive About Incentives?." Journal of Financial Economics 85 (2): 457-489.

Mullainathan, Sendhil, Markus Noeth, and Antoinette Schoar. 2012. "The Market for Financial Advice: An Audit Study." National Bureau of Economic Research Working Paper 17929.

Prentice, Robert A. 2011. "Moral Equilibrium: Stock Brokers and the Limits of Disclosure." *Wisconsin Law Review*: 1059.

Securities and Exchange Commission (SEC). 2007. "Protecting Senior Investors: Report of Examinations of Securities Firms Providing `Free Lunch' Sales Seminar." http://www.sec.gov/spotlight/seniors/freelunchreport.pdf.

—. 2011. "Study on Investment Advisers and Broker-Dealers." http://www.sec.gov/news/studies/2011/913studyfinal.pdf.

Turner, John A. and Dana M. Muir. 2013. "The Market for Financial Advisers." In Olivia S. Mitchell and Kent Smetters (Ed.): *The Market for Retirement Financial Advice.* Oxford University Press, 13-45.

Vanguard. 2014. "How America Saves 2014: A Report on Vanguard 2013 Defined Contribution Plan Data." https://pressroom.vanguard.com/content/nonindexed/How_America_Saves_2014.pdf.